YOUR NAME & MORE
IN FILET CROCHET

TABLE OF CONTENTS

GENERAL INSTRUCTIONS 2

1. INITIAL DESIGN 3

2. TABLE RUNNER 6

3. WALL HANGING 10

4. NAME DESIGN A 12

5. NAME DESIGN B 14

GENERAL INSTRUCTIONS

ABBREVIATIONS

ch(s)	chain(s)
dc	double crochet(s)
mm	millimeters
sc	single crochet(s)
sp(s)	space(s)
st(s)	stitch(es)
YO	yarn over

★ — work instructions following ★ as many **more** times as indicated in addition to the first time.

( ) — work enclosed instructions **as many** times as specified by the number immediately following **or** contains explanatory remarks.

colon (:) — the number(s) given after a colon at the end of a row or round denote(s) the number of stitches you should have on that row or round.

GAUGE

Exact gauge is **essential** for proper size. Before beginning your project, make the sample swatch given in the individual instructions in the thread and hook specified. After completing the swatch, measure it, counting your stitches and rows carefully. If your swatch is larger or smaller than specified, **make another, changing hook size to get the correct gauge**. Keep trying until you find the size hook that will give you the specified gauge.

THREAD

The photographed items were made using bedspread weight cotton thread (size 10). Any of the following brands may be used with good results:

Anchor "Mercer Crochet"
DMC "Baroque"
DMC "Cebelia"
DMC "Cordonnet"
DMC "Traditions"
Grandma's Best
J. & P. Coats "Knit-Cro-Sheen"
J. & P. Coats "South Maid"
Lily "Daisy"
Opera

JOINING WITH DC

When instructed to join with a dc, begin with a slip knot on hook. YO, holding loops on hook, insert hook in stitch indicated, YO and pull up a loop (3 loops on hook), (YO and draw through 2 loops on hook) twice.

FREE LOOPS OF A CHAIN

When instructed to work in free loops of a chain, work in loop indicated by arrow ***(Fig. 1)***.

Fig. 1

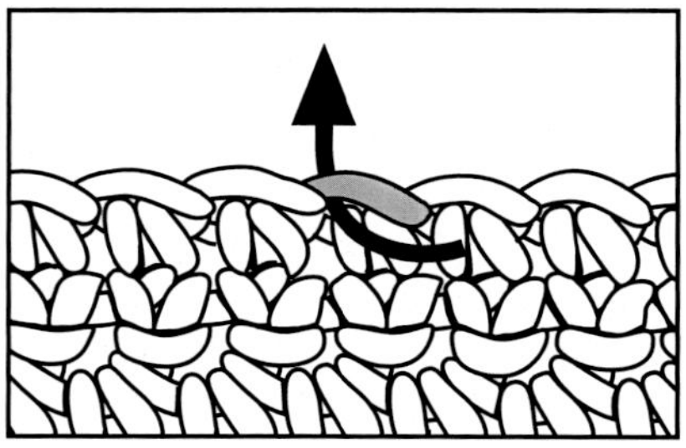

WASHING AND BLOCKING

For a more professional look, pieces should be washed and blocked. Using a mild detergent and warm water and being careful not to rub, twist, or wring, gently squeeze suds through the piece. Rinse several times in cool, clear water. Roll piece in a clean terry towel and gently press out the excess moisture. Lay piece on a flat surface and shape to proper size; where needed, pin in place using rust-proof pins. Allow to dry **completely**.

1. INITIAL DESIGN

Finished Size: 12" w x $11^3/_4$"h
(30.5 cm x 30 cm)

MATERIALS
Bedspread Weight Cotton Thread (size 10):
95 yards **plus** 50-100 yards for initial
Steel crochet hook, size 6 (1.80 mm) **or** size needed for gauge

GAUGE: 36 dc and 16 rows = 4"

Gauge Swatch: 2" square
Ch 20.
Row 1: Dc in fourth ch from hook **(3 skipped chs count as first dc)** and in each ch across: 18 dc.
Rows 2-8: Ch 3 **(counts as first dc)**, turn; dc in next dc and in each dc across.
Finish off.

BASIC CHART STITCHES

BEGINNING BLOCK OVER BLOCK
Ch 3 **(counts as first dc)**, turn; dc in next 3 dc.

BLOCK OVER BLOCK
Dc in next 3 dc.

BLOCK OVER SPACE
2 Dc in next ch-2 sp, dc in next dc.

SPACE OVER BLOCK
Ch 2, skip next 2 dc, dc in next dc.

SPACE OVER SPACE
Ch 2, dc in next dc.

BEGINNING BLOCK DECREASE
Turn; slip st in next 3 dc, ch 3 **(counts as first dc)**.

BEGINNING 2-BLOCK DECREASE
Turn; slip st in next 6 dc, ch 3.

BEGINNING BLOCK INCREASE
Ch 5, turn; dc in fourth ch from hook **(3 skipped chs count as first dc)** and in next ch, dc in next dc.

BEGINNING 2-BLOCK INCREASE
Ch 8, turn; dc in fourth ch from hook **(3 skipped chs count as first dc)** and in next 4 chs, dc in next dc.

ADDING ON DOUBLE CROCHETS
When instructed to add on dc at the end of a row, YO, insert hook into base of last dc ***(Fig. 2)***, YO and pull up a loop (3 loops on hook), YO and draw through one loop on hook, (YO and draw through 2 loops on hook) twice. Repeat as many times as instructed.

Fig. 2

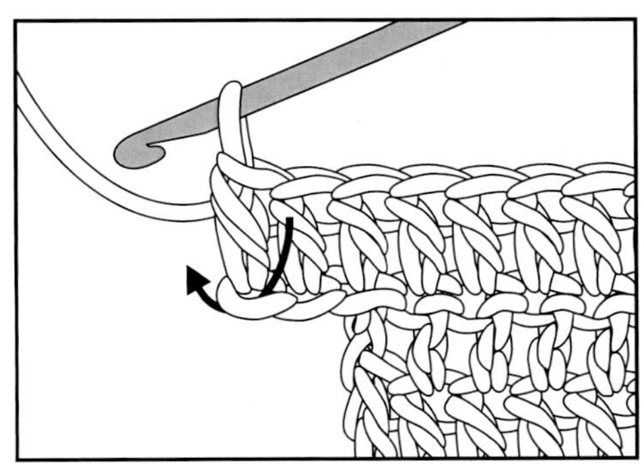

ENDING BLOCK INCREASE
Add on 3 dc ***(Fig. 2)***.

ENDING 2-BLOCK INCREASE
Add on 6 dc ***(Fig. 2)***.

INSTRUCTIONS

Ch 33.

Row 1 (Right side)**:** Dc in fourth ch from hook **(3 skipped chs count as first dc)** and in each ch across: 31 dc.

Note: Loop a short piece of thread around any stitch to mark Row 1 as **right** side.

Row 2: Work Beginning 2-Block Increase, work 10 Spaces, work Ending 2-Block Increase.

Rows 3-5: Follow chart, page 4.

Row 6: Work Beginning Block Increase, work 6 Spaces, work 4 Blocks, ch 6, skip next 5 dc, dc in next dc, work 4 Blocks, work 6 Spaces, work Ending Block Increase.

Row 7: Work Beginning Block Increase, work 7 Spaces, work 3 Blocks, ch 6, sc in next ch-6 sp, ch 6, skip next 3 dc, dc in next dc, work 3 Blocks, work 7 Spaces, work Ending Block Increase.

Row 8: Work Beginning Block Increase, work 4 Spaces, work 2 Blocks, work 3 Spaces, work Block, ch 5, sc in next ch-6 sp, ch 6, sc in next ch-6 sp, ch 5, skip next 3 dc, dc in next dc, work Block, work 3 Spaces, work 2 Blocks, work 4 Spaces, work Ending Block Increase.

Row 9: Work Beginning Block Increase, work 4 Spaces, work 3 Blocks, work 2 Spaces, work 2 Blocks, 3 dc in next ch-5 sp, ch 5, sc in next ch-6 sp, ch 5, 3 dc in next ch-5 sp, dc in next dc, work 2 Blocks, work 2 Spaces, work 3 Blocks, work 4 Spaces, work Ending Block Increase.

Row 10: Work Beginning Block, (work 3 Spaces, work 3 Blocks) twice, 3 dc in next ch-5 sp, ch 5, 3 dc in next ch-5 sp, dc in next dc, (work 3 Blocks, work 3 Spaces) twice, work Block.

Row 11: Work Beginning Block Increase, work 4 Spaces, work 2 Blocks, work 5 Spaces, work 2 Blocks, work Space, 5 dc in next ch-5 sp, dc in next dc, work Space, work 2 Blocks, work 5 Spaces, work 2 Blocks, work 4 Spaces, work Ending Block Increase.

Rows 12-15: Follow chart.

Rows 16-32: Following chart and matching row numbers, work desired letter from letter chart, page 5, using shaded area and center point as a guide for letter placement.

Rows 33-37: Follow chart.

Row 38: Work Beginning Block Decrease, work Block, work 3 Spaces, work 3 Blocks, work 3 Spaces, work 4 Blocks, ch 6, skip next 5 dc, dc in next dc, work 4 Blocks, work 3 Spaces, work 3 Blocks, work 3 Spaces, work Block.

Row 39: Work Beginning Block, work 4 Spaces, work 3 Blocks, work 2 Spaces, work 3 Blocks, ch 6, sc in next ch-6 sp, ch 6, skip next 3 dc, dc in next dc, work 3 Blocks, work 2 Spaces, work 3 Blocks, work 4 Spaces, work Block.

Row 40: Work Beginning Block Decrease, work Block, work 4 Spaces, work 2 Blocks, work 3 Spaces, work Block, ch 5, sc in next ch-6 sp, ch 6, sc in next ch-6 sp, ch 5, skip next 3 dc, dc in next dc, work Block, work 3 Spaces, work 2 Blocks, work 4 Spaces, work Block.

Row 41: Work Beginning Block Decrease, work Block, work 7 Spaces, work 2 Blocks, 3 dc in next ch-5 sp, ch 5, sc in next ch-6 sp, ch 5, 3 dc in next ch-5 sp, dc in next dc, work 2 Blocks, work 7 Spaces, work Block.

Row 42: Work Beginning Block Decrease, work Block, work 6 Spaces, work 3 Blocks, 3 dc in next ch-5 sp, ch 5, 3 dc in next ch-5 sp, dc in next dc, work 3 Blocks, work 6 Spaces, work Block.

Row 43: Work Beginning Block Decrease, work Block, work 6 Spaces, work 2 Blocks, work Space, 5 dc in next ch-5 sp, dc in next dc, work Space, work 2 Blocks, work 6 Spaces, work Block.

Rows 44-47: Follow chart.

Finish off.

See Washing and Blocking, page 2.

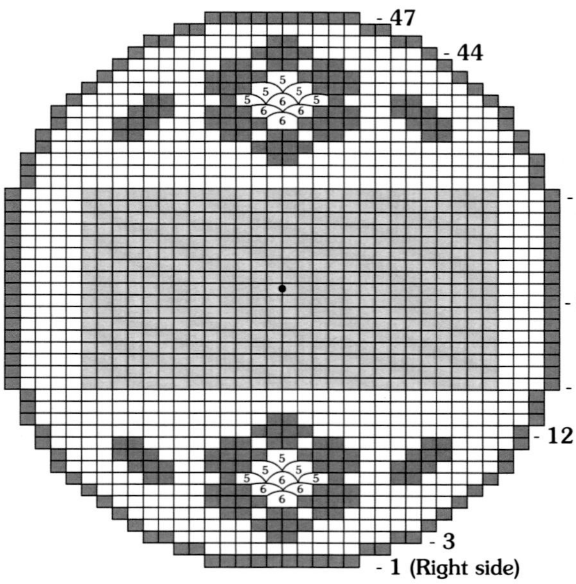

KEY

- Block

- Space

On **odd-numbered** rows, follow chart from **right** to **left**; on **even-numbered** rows, follow chart from **left** to **right**.

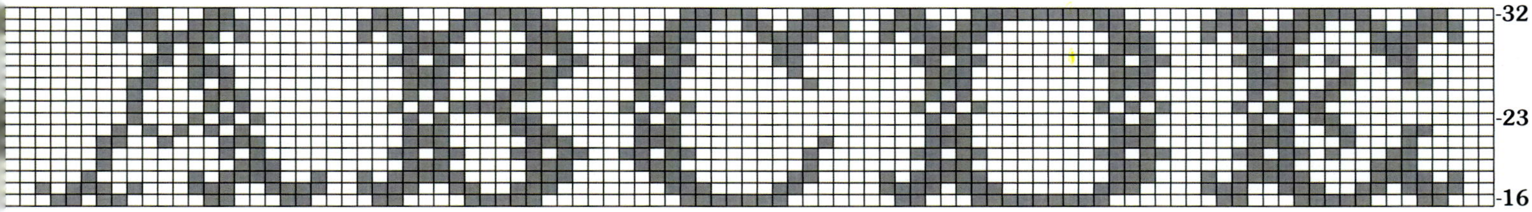
-32
-23
-16

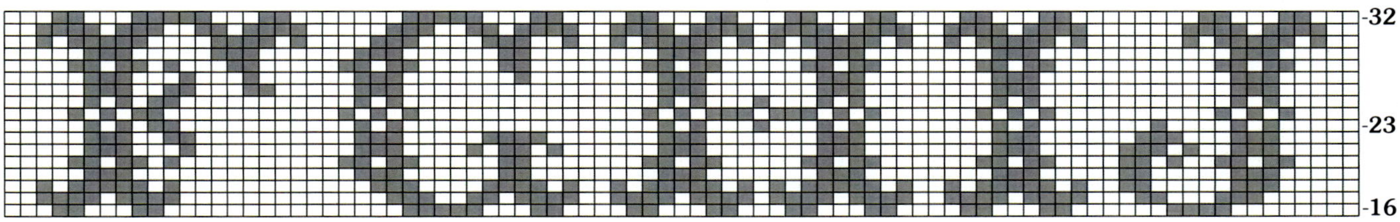
-32
-23
-16

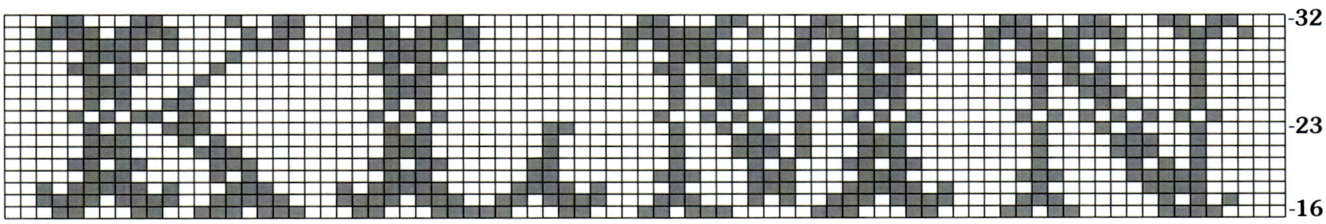
-32
-23
-16

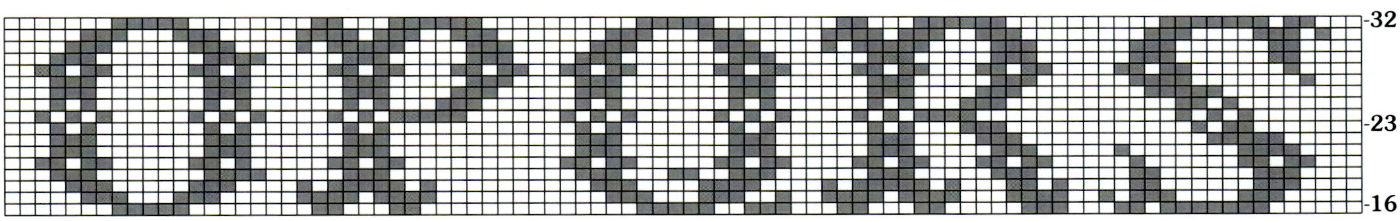
-32
-23
-16

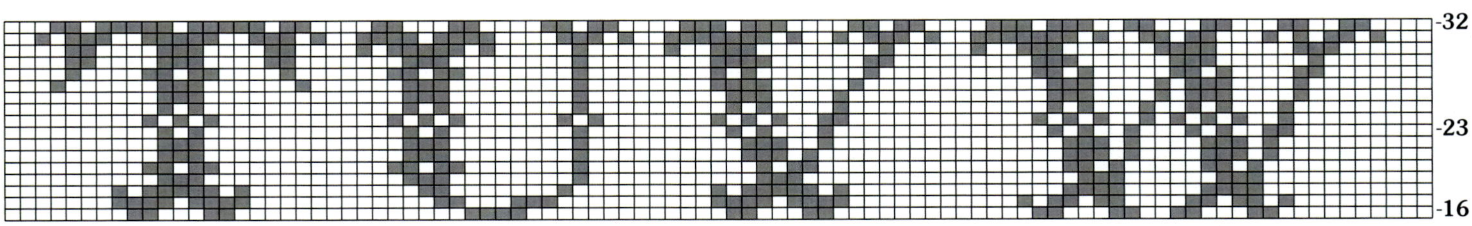
-32
-23
-16

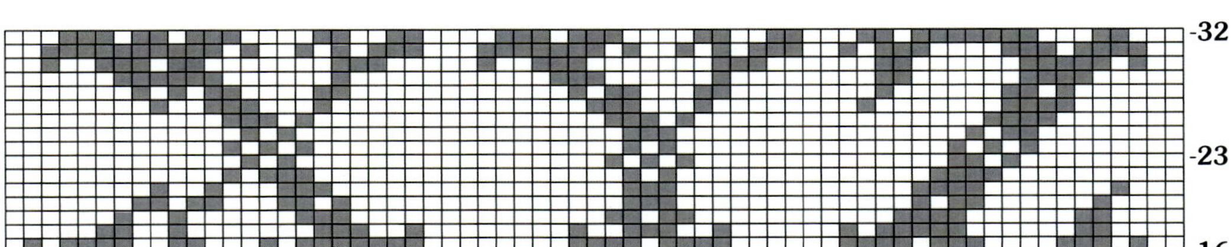
-32
-23
-16

2. TABLE RUNNER

Finished Size: 48"w x 19¼"h
(122 cm x 49 cm)

MATERIALS

Bedspread Weight Cotton Thread (size 10): 1,355 yards

Steel crochet hook, size 6 (1.80 mm) **or** size needed for gauge

GAUGE: 36 dc and 16 rows = 4"
Gauge Swatch: 2" square
Ch 20.
Row 1: Dc in fourth ch from hook **(3 skipped chs count as first dc)** and in each ch across: 18 dc.
Rows 2-8: Ch 3 **(counts as first dc)**, turn; dc in next dc and in each dc across.
Finish off.

BASIC CHART STITCHES

BEGINNING BLOCK OVER BLOCK
Ch 3, turn; dc in next 3 dc.

BLOCK OVER BLOCK
Dc in next 3 dc.

BLOCK OVER SPACE
2 Dc in next ch-2 sp, dc in next dc.

SPACE OVER BLOCK
Ch 2, skip next 2 dc, dc in next dc.

SPACE OVER SPACE
Ch 2, dc in next dc.

INSTRUCTIONS

Ch 435.

Row 1 (Right side)**:** Dc in fourth ch from hook **(3 skipped chs count as first dc)** and in each ch across: 433 dc.

Note: Loop a short piece of thread around any stitch to mark Row 1 as **right** side.

Rows 2 and 3: Ch 3 **(counts as first dc, now and throughout)**, turn; dc in next dc and in each dc across.

Row 4: Work Beginning Block, work 3 Blocks, work 9 Spaces, work 2 Blocks, (work 21 Spaces, work 2 Blocks) 4 times, work 22 Spaces, work 2 Blocks, work 9 Spaces, work 4 Blocks.

Rows 5-77: Follow chart, page 7.

Finish off.

See Washing and Blocking, page 2.

KEY
- **Block**
- **Space**

On **odd-numbered** rows, follow chart from **right** to **left**;
on **even-numbered** rows, follow chart from **left** to **right**.

2

5
SULLIVAN

3. WALL HANGING

Finished Size: $28^1/_2$"w x $25^1/_4$"h (72.5 cm x 64 cm) (excluding loops)

MATERIALS

Bedspread Weight Cotton Thread (size 10): 875 yards
Steel crochet hook, size 6 (1.80 mm) **or** size needed for gauge
$^1/_2$" Wood Pole Set cut to $28^1/_2$" length

GAUGE: 36 dc and 16 rows = 4"
Gauge Swatch: 2" square
Ch 20.
Row 1: Dc in fourth ch from hook **(3 skipped chs count as first dc)** and in each ch across: 18 dc.
Rows 2-8: Ch 3 **(counts as first dc)**, turn; dc in next dc and in each dc across.
Finish off.

BASIC CHART STITCHES

BEGINNING BLOCK OVER BLOCK
Ch 3 **(counts as first dc, now and throughout)**, turn; dc in next 3 dc.

BLOCK OVER BLOCK
Dc in next 3 dc.

BLOCK OVER SPACE
2 Dc in next ch-2 sp, dc in next dc.

SPACE OVER BLOCK
Ch 2, skip next 2 dc, dc in next dc.

SPACE OVER SPACE
Ch 2, dc in next dc.

INSTRUCTIONS

Ch 258.

Row 1 (Right side)**:** Dc in fourth ch from hook **(3 skipped chs count as first dc)** and in each ch across: 256 dc.

Note: Loop a short piece of thread around any stitch to mark Row 1 as **right** side.

Row 2: Work Beginning Block, (work Block, work Space) across to last 2 Blocks, work 2 Blocks.

Rows 3-21: Follow chart, page 11.

Rows 22-27: Following chart and matching row numbers, work desired numbers from number chart, using shaded area and center point as a guide for number placement and allowing one space between each number.

Rows 28-101: Follow chart; at end of Row 101, do **not** finish off.

HANGING LOOPS

Row 1: Ch 3, turn; dc in next 3 dc, ★ ch 28, skip next 3 dc, dc in next 4 dc; repeat from ★ across: 148 dc and 36 loops.

Row 2: Ch 3, turn; dc in next 3 dc, ★ ch 12, slip st in next loop, ch 12, dc in next 4 dc; repeat from ★ across; finish off.

See Washing and Blocking, page 2.

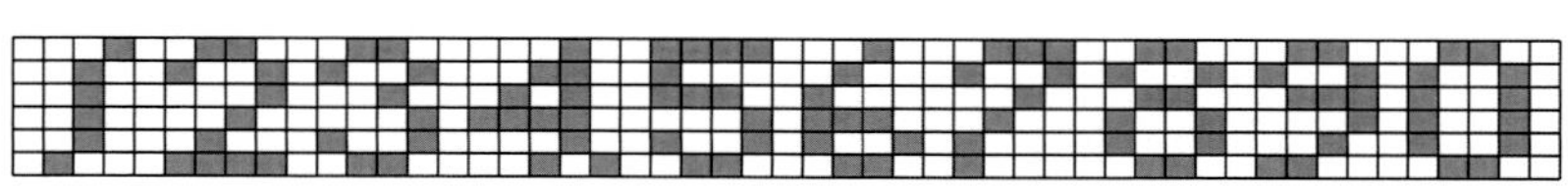

On **odd-numbered** rows, follow chart from **right** to **left**;
on **even-numbered** rows, follow chart from **left** to **right**.

KEY

- **Block** (shaded square)
- **Space** (blank square)

4. NAME DESIGN A

Finished Size: 7"h (18 cm)

MATERIALS

Bedspread Weight Cotton Thread (size 10): 50 yards **plus** 15-30 yards for **each** letter
Steel crochet hook, size 6 (1.80 mm) **or** size needed for gauge

GAUGE: 36 dc and 16 rows = 4"
Gauge Swatch: 2" square
Ch 20.
Row 1: Dc in fourth ch from hook **(3 skipped chs count as first dc)** and in each ch across: 18 dc.
Rows 2-8: Ch 3 **(counts as first dc)**, turn; dc in next dc and in each dc across.
Finish off.

BASIC CHART STITCHES

BEGINNING BLOCK OVER BLOCK
Ch 3 **(counts as first dc)**, turn; dc in next 3 dc.

BLOCK OVER BLOCK
Dc in next 3 dc.

BLOCK OVER SPACE
2 Dc in next ch-2 sp, dc in next dc.

SPACE OVER BLOCK
Ch 2, skip next 2 dc, dc in next dc.

SPACE OVER SPACE
Ch 2, dc in next dc.

BEGINNING BLOCK DECREASE
Turn; slip st in next 3 dc, ch 3 **(counts as first dc)**.

BEGINNING 2-BLOCK DECREASE
Turn; slip st in next 6 dc, ch 3.

INSTRUCTIONS

Ch 66.

Foundation Row (Right side)**:** Dc in fourth ch from hook **(3 skipped chs count as first dc)** and in next 2 chs, ch 2, ★ skip next 2 chs, dc in next ch, ch 2; repeat from ★ across to last 6 chs, skip next 2 chs, dc in last 4 chs: 2 Blocks and 19 Spaces.

Note: Loop a short piece of thread around any stitch to mark Foundation Row as **right** side.

Working one row of Spaces between each letter, work desired letters from chart, page 13, working one Block and 5 Spaces before **top** of each letter.

After working last letter, do **not** finish off.

FIRST END

Rows 1-3: Work Beginning Block, work Spaces across to last Block, work Block: 2 Blocks and 19 Spaces.

Rows 4-12: Follow End Chart.

Finish off.

SECOND END

Row 1: With **wrong** side facing and working in free loops of beginning ch ***(Fig. 1, page 2)***, join thread with dc in ch at base of first dc ***(see Joining With Dc, page 2)***; dc in next 3 chs, ch 2, ★ skip next 2 chs, dc in next ch, ch 2; repeat from ★ across to last 6 chs, skip next 2 chs, dc in last 4 chs: 2 Blocks and 19 Spaces.

Beginning with Row 3, complete same as First End.

See Washing and Blocking, page 2.

END CHART

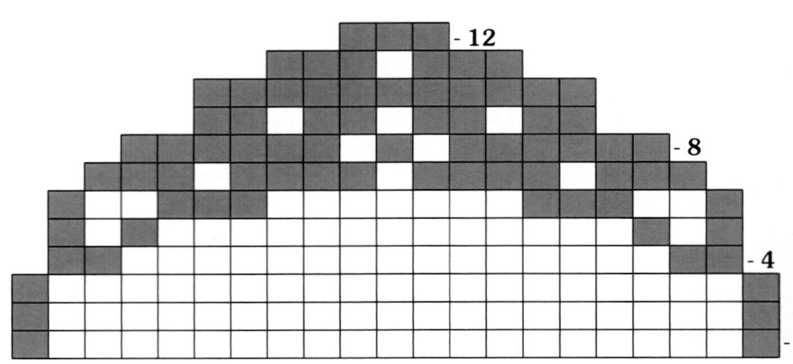

KEY

- Block

- Space

On **right** side rows, follow chart from **right** to **left**; on **wrong** side rows, follow chart from **left** to **right**.

5. NAME DESIGN B

Finished Size: 9¾"h (25 cm)

MATERIALS

Bedspread Weight Cotton Thread (size 10):
95 yards **plus** 20-45 yards for **each** letter
Steel crochet hook, size 6 (1.80 mm) **or** size needed for gauge

GAUGE: 36 dc and 16 rows = 4"
Gauge Swatch: 2" square
Ch 20.
Row 1: Dc in fourth ch from hook **(3 skipped chs count as first dc)** and in each ch across: 18 dc.
Rows 2-8: Ch 3 **(counts as first dc)**, turn; dc in next dc and in each dc across.
Finish off.

BASIC CHART STITCHES

BEGINNING BLOCK OVER BLOCK
Ch 3 **(counts as first dc, now and throughout)**, turn; dc in next 3 dc.

BEGINNING BLOCK OVER SPACE
Ch 3, turn; 2 dc in next ch-2 sp, dc in next dc.

BEGINNING SPACE OVER BLOCK
Ch 5 **(counts as first dc plus ch 2, now and throughout)**, turn; skip next 2 dc, dc in next dc.

BEGINNING SPACE OVER SPACE
Ch 5, turn; dc in next dc.

BLOCK OVER BLOCK
Dc in next 3 dc.

BLOCK OVER SPACE
2 Dc in next ch-2 sp, dc in next dc.

SPACE OVER BLOCK
Ch 2, skip next 2 dc, dc in next dc.

SPACE OVER SPACE
Ch 2, dc in next dc.

BEGINNING BLOCK DECREASE
Turn; slip st in next 3 dc, ch 3.

BEGINNING 3-BLOCK DECREASE
Turn; slip st in next 9 dc, ch 3.

INSTRUCTIONS

Ch 90.

Foundation Row (Right side)**:** Dc in fourth ch from hook **(3 skipped chs count as first dc)** and in next 2 chs, ch 2, ★ skip next 2 chs, dc in next ch, ch 2; repeat from ★ across to last 6 chs, skip next 2 chs, dc in last 4 chs: 2 Blocks and 27 Spaces.

Note: Loop a short piece of thread around any stitch to mark Foundation Row as **right** side.

Working two rows of Spaces between each letter, work desired letters from chart, page 15, working one Block and 8 Spaces before **top** of each letter.

After working last letter, do **not** finish off.

FIRST END

Rows 1 and 2: Work Beginning Block, work Spaces across to last Block, work Block: 2 Blocks and 27 Spaces.

Rows 3-14: Follow End Chart.

Row 15: Turn; slip st in next 3 dc, slip st in next 2 chs and in next dc, ch 3, work 3 Blocks, work 2 Spaces, work Block, work 3 Spaces, work Block, work 2 Spaces, work 3 Blocks.

Row 16: Turn; slip st in next 9 dc, slip st in next 2 chs and in next dc, ch 5, dc in next dc, work Space, work 3 Blocks, work 2 Spaces; finish off.

SECOND END

Row 1: With **wrong** side facing and working in free loops of beginning ch ***(Fig. 1, page 2)***, join thread with dc in ch at base of first dc ***(see Joining With Dc, page 2)***; dc in next 3 chs, ch 2, ★ skip next 2 chs, dc in next ch, ch 2; repeat from ★ across to last 6 chs, skip next 2 chs, dc in last 4 chs: 2 Blocks and 27 Spaces.

Beginning with Row 3, complete same as First End.

See Washing and Blocking, page 2.

END CHART

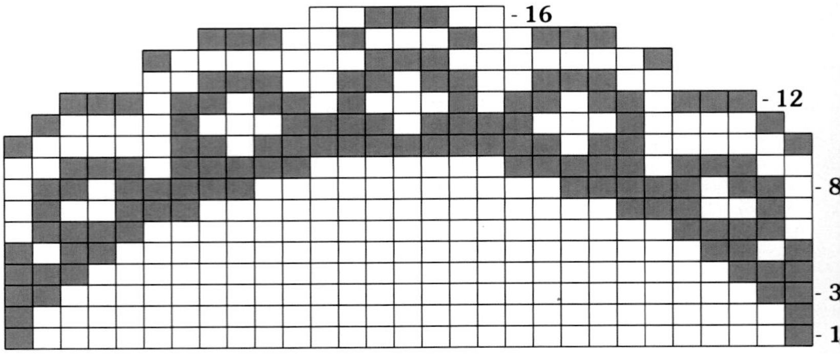

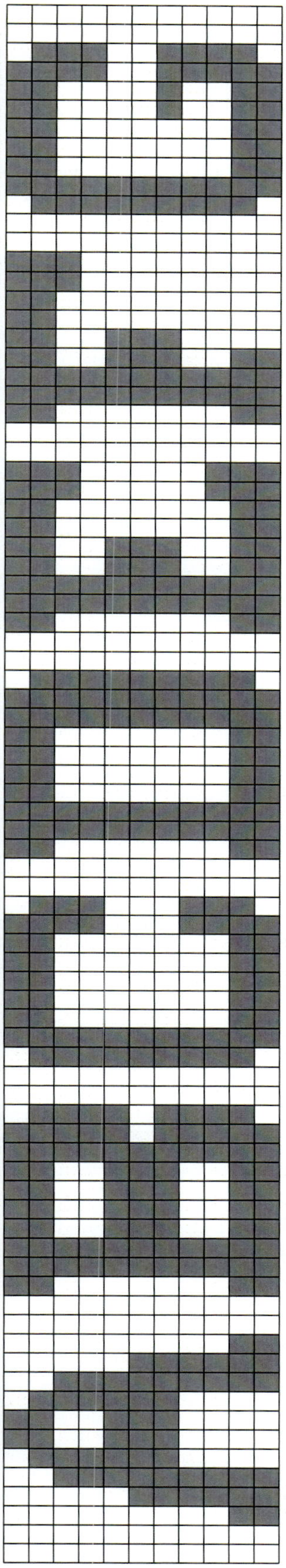

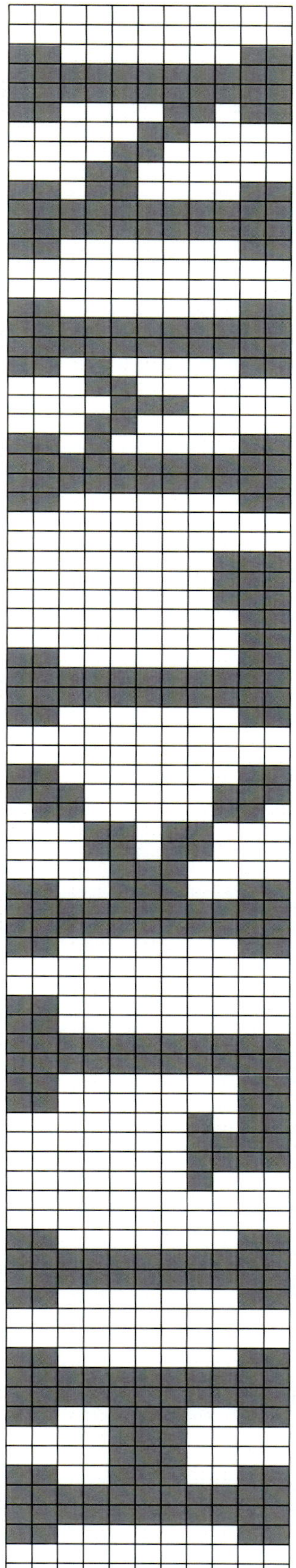

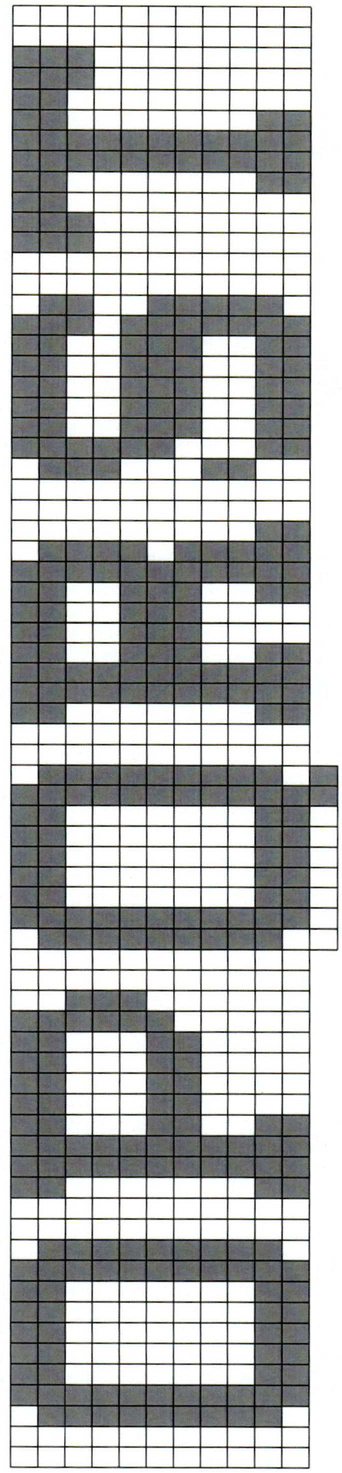

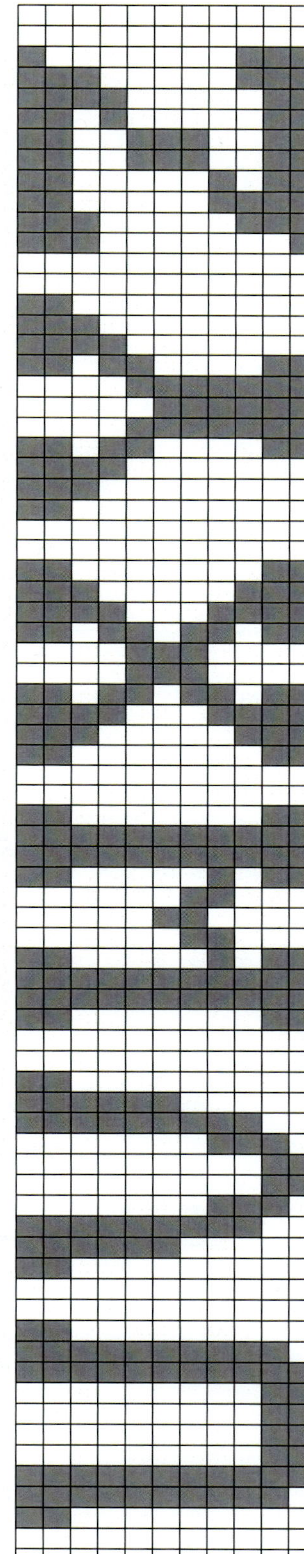

KEY

- Block

- Space

On **right** side rows, follow chart from **right** to **left**; on **wrong** side rows, follow chart from **left** to **right**.

We have made every effort to ensure that these instructions are accurate and complete. We cannot, however, be responsible for human error, typographical mistakes, or variations in individual work.

Items made and instructions tested by Marianna Crowder, Jean Hall, Dale Potter, and Carla Rains.

Production Team: Writer - Valesha Kirksey; Technical Editor - Linda Luder; Artist - Katie Murphy; and Photo Stylist - Sondra Daniel.

Made in U.S.A.